System Design Interview

An Insider's Guide

Book 2

TABLE OF CONTENTS

Introduction

Delving Deeper into Modern System Design Principles

In today's ever-evolving technological landscape, the intricacies of system design have expanded far beyond foundational concepts, presenting challenges and opportunities alike. System design now permeates virtually every aspect of our digital lives, from the e-commerce platforms we frequent to the IoT devices we deploy in our homes. This introduction seeks to set the stage for a profound exploration into the cutting-edge principles and methodologies that define modern system design.

The Evolution of System Design

Historically, system design was primarily concerned with creating monolithic applications where all components existed within a confined environment. As technology advanced and user needs grew, the shift moved towards distributed systems to handle scalability, reliability, and performance requirements. This evolution has paved the way for a plethora of novel architectures and design patterns, from microservices to serverless computing.

Yet, as we've transitioned to these more complex ecosystems, the fundamental principles of system design have remained unchanged. They continue to be anchored in ensuring efficiency, scalability, resilience, and maintainability. However, their application has become more nuanced, requiring system designers to possess not only a deep technical acumen but also an understanding of user behavior, business needs, and even geopolitical considerations.

The Challenges of Modern System Design

Modern system design is fraught with challenges, many of which arise from the sheer volume of data being generated and the demand for near-instantaneous processing. Consider real-time analytics, where vast streams of data must be ingested, processed, and visualized in the blink of an eye. Or take the example of AI training infrastructures, which demand robust architectures to handle extensive computational loads.

Adding to this complexity is the growing importance of cybersecurity. With the proliferation of digital platforms, the potential for security breaches has grown exponentially. Designing systems that are not only efficient and scalable but also secure has become paramount.

Furthermore, with the rise of global platforms, system designers must account for cross-border data transfers, varying regulatory landscapes, and diverse user bases with unique requirements. Thus, modern system design transcends pure technical challenges, delving into the realm of global policy, ethics, and user experience.

The Significance of Scalability

One of the pivotal aspects of modern system design is scalability. Scalability, in essence, is the system's ability to handle increased load gracefully. This could mean serving millions of users concurrently on a social media platform or processing billions of transactions on an e-commerce site during peak sales.

While vertical scalability (adding more power to existing machines) was once the default approach, horizontal scalability (adding more machines to the system) has become the norm, especially with the advent of cloud computing. Distributed systems, by their very nature, are designed with scalability in mind, ensuring that resources can be added or removed dynamically based on demand.

User Experience at the Heart of Design

Another paradigm shift in system design is the central role of user experience. No longer is it enough for a system to be merely functional; it must also deliver a seamless and intuitive experience. From the latency of a video streaming service to the personalization algorithms of a shopping platform, user experience can make or break a digital product.

This heightened focus on user experience demands that system designers collaborate closely with UX designers, product managers, and even behavioral psychologists. The goal is to anticipate user needs and design systems that are not only robust but also user-friendly.

Anticipating the Future

As we delve into the subsequent chapters, we'll explore in detail the design principles behind various contemporary systems, from ride-sharing platforms to blockchain networks. But beyond understanding the current landscape, a proficient system designer must also anticipate the future.

Emerging technologies such as quantum computing, edge computing, and neuromorphic engineering are poised to redefine the very fabric of system design. Preparing for these shifts, understanding their implications, and harnessing their potential will be vital.

In conclusion, system design is an ever-evolving field, requiring continuous learning and adaptation. As we embark on this journey through "System Design Interview – An Insider's Guide vol3," we aim to equip readers with the knowledge and tools necessary to navigate the challenges and opportunities of modern system design. Whether you're preparing for an interview, looking to deepen your understanding, or simply curious about the digital systems that power our world, this guide seeks to be a comprehensive resource for all your needs.

Chapter 1: Geo-Location Based Recommendations

Harnessing Location Data for Personalized User Experiences

1.1 The Power of Location Data

In our interconnected digital era, geo-location data has emerged as a potent tool in driving personalized user experiences. From suggesting nearby restaurants on a food delivery app to curating region-specific news feeds, location data enhances the relevance and utility of digital platforms. This chapter delves into the intricacies of building systems that effectively harness this data, ensuring both accuracy and user privacy.

1.2 Fundamental Components of Geo-Location Systems

Before diving deep into design strategies, it's crucial to understand the core components that constitute geo-location systems:

- **GPS (Global Positioning System):** A satellite-based navigation system, which allows any device with a GPS receiver to determine its precise location (latitude, longitude, and altitude) anywhere on Earth.

- **Cell Tower Triangulation:** In the absence of GPS, mobile devices can use nearby cell towers to approximate their location. This method is less accurate than GPS but works well in densely populated areas.
- **Wi-Fi Positioning Systems (WPS):** Devices can also determine their location using the names and strengths of nearby Wi-Fi networks. This is particularly useful indoors where GPS signals may be weak or unavailable.
- **Geofencing:** A feature that uses the device's location to define geographical boundaries. When the device enters or exits these boundaries, specific predefined actions or notifications can be triggered.

1.3 Design Considerations for Geo-Location Systems

- **Accuracy:** The precision of location data can vary depending on the source. While GPS provides high accuracy, cell tower triangulation and Wi-Fi positioning may offer less precise results. System designers must account for these variations, especially when accuracy is critical, such as in navigation apps.

- **Latency:** Real-time applications, like ride-sharing services, demand rapid location updates. Delays in updating or retrieving location data can degrade user experience and operational efficiency.
- **Scalability:** Popular platforms may need to handle location queries from millions of users simultaneously. The system's architecture must be robust enough to scale with demand without compromising performance.
- **User Privacy:** Handling location data brings significant privacy concerns. Users must be informed about how their data is used, and robust encryption and anonymization techniques should be employed to protect this sensitive information.

1.4 Application and Use Cases

Geo-location systems find applications across various domains:

- **Retail:** Brick-and-mortar stores can send promotional notifications to users when they are nearby, enhancing foot traffic and sales.
- **Healthcare:** In case of emergencies, the nearest hospital or clinic can be quickly identified and navigated to.
- **Entertainment:** Augmented reality games, like Pokémon GO, utilize location data to offer immersive experiences.
- **Logistics:** Package tracking and delivery optimization are greatly enhanced with real-time geo-location capabilities.

1.5 Challenges and Pitfalls

Despite their immense potential, geo-location systems come with their set of challenges:

- **Signal Interference:** Tall buildings, tunnels, and even atmospheric conditions can interfere with GPS signals, leading to inaccurate location readings.
- **Battery Consumption:** Continuous location tracking, especially using GPS, can be battery-intensive, impacting device performance.

- **Data Overhead:** Storing, processing, and transmitting vast amounts of location data requires significant computational and storage resources.
- **Legal and Regulatory Issues:** Different jurisdictions have varying regulations about collecting, storing, and using location data, necessitating compliance checks in system design.

1.6 Looking Ahead

As technologies like 5G and edge computing become mainstream, geo-location systems' capabilities are poised to expand. Future systems might offer even more granular location data, enabling hyper-personalized experiences. However, with increased capabilities come heightened responsibilities, especially around user privacy and data security.

In conclusion, geo-location based recommendations stand at the intersection of technology, user experience, and ethics. Designing effective and responsible systems in this domain requires a blend of technical prowess, user-centric thinking, and a deep understanding of the broader societal implications. As we move forward, the challenge for system designers is not just to harness the power of location data but to do so in a way that respects user agency and safeguards their trust.

Chapter 2: Social Media Feed Generation

Efficiently Delivering Relevant Content to Millions

2.1 Introduction to Feed Systems

Social media platforms revolve around the user's feed—a curated stream of content tailored to an individual's preferences, behaviors, and network. The generation and delivery of this feed, especially in real-time and at scale, presents a complex set of technical challenges. In this chapter, we'll navigate the intricacies of creating an efficient and responsive feed generation system.

2.2 Components of a Feed System

Understanding the fundamental components is essential to grasp the complexity of feed generation:

- **Content Repository:** A vast storage system that holds all user-generated content, including text posts, images, videos, and more.

- **User Profiles:** Databases storing user preferences, behaviors, and connections.
- **Feed Generation Engine:** An algorithmic system that selects and arranges content for individual user feeds based on multiple factors.
- **Caching Systems:** These hold frequently accessed content to reduce the load on primary databases and provide faster user access.

2.3 Principles of Feed Generation

- **Relevance:** The primary goal is to deliver content deemed relevant to the user. This could be based on previous interactions, liked content, or connections' activities.
- **Timeliness:** Recent content often takes precedence, ensuring users see fresh updates and news.
- **Diversity:** To prevent feed monotony, a diverse mix of content types and sources is essential.
- **User Feedback Loops:** Users' interactions with their feed (likes, shares, hides) provide vital feedback, further refining the feed generation process.

2.4 Technical Challenges and Solutions

- **Latency:** With users expecting real-time updates, minimizing latency is crucial. Solutions include efficient indexing, optimized query patterns, and robust caching mechanisms.
- **Scalability:** Social media platforms can have billions of users. Distributed databases, horizontal scaling, and stateless application design are techniques employed to manage such vast user bases.
- **Data Freshness:** Ensuring the most recent content is available requires real-time data processing and streaming systems, like Apache Kafka.
- **Ranking and Personalization:** Advanced machine learning models can be employed to rank content based on predicted user engagement. These models need to be regularly updated to capture evolving user behaviors.

2.5 Ethical and Societal Implications

- **Echo Chambers:** Over-personalization can lead users into echo chambers, where they only see content aligning with their existing beliefs. Designing for diversity and serendipity in content discovery is essential.

- **Privacy:** User data, including behavior and interactions, are pivotal for feed generation. Protecting this data and ensuring ethical usage is paramount.
- **Misinformation:** The viral nature of content on social media can spread misinformation rapidly. Feed algorithms must be designed with safeguards against such propagation.

2.6 Innovations in Feed Generation

- **Collaborative Filtering:** Utilizing user behavior similarities to predict and recommend content.
- **Semantic Analysis:** Delving into the meaning of content, ensuring a deeper understanding and better content matching.
- **Augmented Reality (AR) and Virtual Reality (VR) Integration:** As AR and VR become more mainstream, feeds might incorporate immersive content, demanding new design paradigms.

2.7 Conclusion

The feed is the heart of any social media platform. Its generation is a dance of technology, user psychology, and societal impact. As platforms grow and evolve, the challenges of delivering a relevant, engaging, and responsible feed only intensify. System designers, therefore, must continuously adapt, innovate, and most importantly, keep the user at the center of their design ethos. The coming chapters will further delve into other complex systems, but the principles of user-centricity, efficiency, and responsibility will remain consistent themes.

Chapter 3: Cloud-Based Storage Solutions

Crafting Robust, Scalable, and Secure Data Repositories in the Cloud

3.1 Understanding Cloud Storage

The rise of cloud computing has fundamentally changed how businesses approach data storage. No longer confined to physical on-site servers, data can now be securely stored, accessed, and managed on cloud platforms. This chapter explores the architecture, benefits, and challenges of cloud-based storage solutions.

3.2 Key Components of Cloud Storage Systems

- **Storage Servers:** Physical servers located in data centers worldwide that hold the actual data. They often utilize redundant array configurations to safeguard against data loss.
- **Data Redundancy and Distribution Layers:** Systems that replicate data across multiple servers or even multiple data

centers, ensuring availability and durability.

- **API Layer:** Provides interfaces for users and applications to interact with, manage, and retrieve stored data.
- **Access Control Systems:** Manage permissions and ensure that only authorized users can access specific data.

3.3 Types of Cloud Storage Solutions

- **Object Storage:** Best suited for unstructured data like multimedia. Examples include Amazon S3 and Google Cloud Storage.
- **File Storage:** Designed for hierarchical data and file systems, such as those needed by traditional applications.
- **Block Storage:** Used primarily by databases and provides raw storage capabilities, acting like traditional disk drives.
- **Cold or Archive Storage:** Optimized for long-term storage where immediate access is not a priority. It's a cost-effective solution for data that is accessed infrequently.

3.4 Advantages of Cloud-Based Storage

- **Scalability:** Allows businesses to scale storage needs up or down based on demand without significant upfront investments.
- **Durability and Availability:** Built-in redundancies ensure high data durability, and global distribution ensures data availability.
- **Cost-Effectiveness:** Businesses can often reduce costs due to the pay-as-you-use model of many cloud storage providers.
- **Flexibility:** Easy integration with other cloud services, from machine learning platforms to web hosting.

3.5 Technical Challenges and Solutions

- **Latency:** Accessing data in the cloud can introduce latency, especially if the data center is geographically distant. Solutions include content delivery networks (CDNs) and edge caching.
- **Data Security:** Storing data off-site might pose security concerns. Encryption, both at rest and in transit, along with robust access controls, can mitigate risks.

- **Data Sovereignty:** Different countries have varying regulations about where data can be stored, especially personal or sensitive data. To comply, cloud providers often offer region-specific storage solutions.
- **Cost Management:** While cloud storage can be cost-effective, mismanagement (like not deleting unused data) can lead to unforeseen expenses.

3.6 Innovations in Cloud Storage

- **Multi-Cloud Strategies:** Using multiple cloud providers to ensure redundancy, optimize costs, and avoid vendor lock-in.
- **Intelligent Tiering:** Systems that automatically move data between storage tiers based on access patterns, optimizing costs.
- **Serverless Storage Solutions:** Allows developers to interact with storage without managing the underlying infrastructure.

3.7 Ethical and Societal Implications

- **Environmental Impact:** Large cloud data centers consume significant power.

Sustainable energy sources and efficient cooling solutions are becoming pivotal.

- **Monopolization Concerns:** A few major players dominate the cloud industry. Relying heavily on a single provider can raise concerns about monopolization and associated risks.

3.8 Conclusion

Cloud-based storage solutions have revolutionized how businesses, big and small, approach data. They offer unmatched flexibility, scalability, and resilience. However, navigating the cloud landscape requires a blend of technical knowledge, strategic planning, and ethical considerations. As the digital universe continues to expand, the importance of robust, efficient, and responsible cloud storage solutions becomes ever more paramount. Future chapters will further delve into other cloud-based systems, emphasizing the synergy of technology and strategy in modern digital infrastructures.

Chapter 4: Advanced Load Balancing Techniques

Optimizing Traffic Distribution for High-Performance Web Infrastructure

4.1 Grasping the Essence of Load Balancing

At the foundation of every high-performing web service lies an unsung hero: the load balancer. Its task is to distribute incoming network traffic across multiple servers, ensuring no single server is overwhelmed. This chapter sheds light on the nuances of advanced load balancing, its methods, and its paramount role in maintaining service reliability.

4.2 Core Principles of Load Balancing

- **Distribution:** Efficiently allocate incoming requests across a pool of servers based on various strategies.
- **Redundancy:** Ensure service availability even when some servers or components fail.
- **Scalability:** Seamlessly handle varying traffic loads, scaling resources up or down as required.

- **Latency Minimization:** Direct traffic in a manner that reduces response times for the end-user.

4.3 Techniques and Types of Load Balancers

- **Round Robin:** A straightforward method, where each server is chosen in rotation.
- **Least Connections:** Directs traffic to the server with the fewest active connections.
- **IP Hash:** Determines the server destination based on the IP address of the client or another key piece of information, ensuring a consistent mapping.
- **Layer 4 vs. Layer 7 Load Balancing:** While Layer 4 operates at the transport level (TCP/UDP), Layer 7 operates at the application level, allowing for more sophisticated distribution decisions based on content type, URL, and other HTTP header information.

4.4 Hardware vs. Software Load Balancers

- **Hardware Load Balancers:** Dedicated physical devices optimized for distributing network traffic. They offer high performance but can be expensive and less flexible.

- **Software Load Balancers:** Virtual instances running on standard hardware. While they might be less performant than dedicated hardware for extreme loads, they offer unparalleled flexibility, scalability, and are often more cost-effective.

4.5 Challenges in Advanced Load Balancing

- **Session Persistence:** Some applications require that a user's session remains on a single server. Achieving this persistence while balancing loads can be challenging.
- **Dynamic Infrastructure:** With the rise of containerization and orchestration tools like Kubernetes, infrastructure can change rapidly. Load balancers must adapt in real-time.
- **Multi-Region Balancing:** For global applications, directing traffic to the nearest data center or region to minimize latency becomes crucial.
- **Security:** Load balancers can be targets for attacks, including DDoS attacks.

Implementing security measures without compromising performance is pivotal.

4.6 Innovative Trends in Load Balancing

- **Machine Learning-Driven Balancing:** Utilizing AI and ML to predict traffic patterns and optimize load distribution proactively.
- **Service Mesh Architectures:** For microservices-based applications, service meshes offer fine-grained load balancing at the service level.
- **Multi-Cloud Load Balancing:** Distributing traffic across servers in different cloud providers to enhance redundancy and reliability.

4.7 Ethical and Regulatory Considerations

- **Data Localization:** Balancing loads across international borders might conflict with regulations that dictate where data about citizens can be stored and processed.
- **Fairness in Service:** Ensuring that load balancing doesn't prioritize one set of users or clients over another, especially in

contexts where equal access is legally or ethically mandated.

4.8 Conclusion

Load balancing stands as a cornerstone of resilient and responsive web infrastructures. Its evolution, from simple round-robin methods to sophisticated machine learning-driven approaches, mirrors the growth and complexity of the digital world. As web services continue to scale and diversify, the techniques and strategies around load balancing will remain central to the discourse on web performance and reliability. The subsequent chapters will further explore components that, in conjunction with load balancers, create the symphony of seamless digital experiences.

Chapter 5: Modern Data Streaming Platforms

Real-time Data Processing and Analysis for Dynamic Business Insights

5.1 Introduction to Data Streaming

In today's digital landscape, the ability to process and analyze data in real-time is a competitive advantage for businesses. Data streaming platforms enable this by capturing, processing, and moving vast amounts of data quickly. This chapter dives deep into the anatomy of such platforms, their significance, and the challenges they present.

5.2 The Pillars of Data Streaming

- **Data Ingestion:** The process of collecting and importing data, both in batch and real-time modes, into the streaming platform.
- **Data Processing:** Real-time analysis and transformation of data using complex event processing engines.
- **Data Storage:** Temporarily or persistently storing data for later retrieval and analysis.

- **Data Consumption:** Exporting or serving processed data to various endpoints, be it applications, dashboards, or other systems.

5.3 Core Technologies in the Data Streaming Ecosystem

- **Apache Kafka:** A distributed event streaming platform known for its durability, scalability, and real-time capabilities.
- **Apache Flink:** A stream processing framework that allows for stateful computations over data streams.
- **Amazon Kinesis:** A cloud-native solution offering streaming data capabilities on AWS.
- **Apache Pulsar:** A distributed pub-sub messaging platform designed for high-performance streaming.

5.4 Benefits of Data Streaming Platforms

- **Real-time Decision Making:** Businesses can make data-driven decisions instantly, reacting to market changes, user behaviors, or system anomalies.

- **Enhanced User Experiences:** By processing user data in real-time, applications can offer personalized and dynamic user experiences.
- **Operational Efficiency:** Automated real-time monitoring and alerting can highlight system inefficiencies or issues before they escalate.
- **Data Integration:** Streamlining data from multiple sources provides a unified view of business operations and metrics.

5.5 Challenges and Solutions in Data Streaming

- **Data Integrity:** Ensuring data isn't lost or duplicated during streaming. Solutions include idempotent writes and exactly-once processing semantics.
- **Scalability:** Handling varying data loads requires elastic scaling of resources. Distributed architectures and cloud-native solutions can address this.
- **Latency:** Minimizing the delay between data ingestion and consumption is crucial for real-time applications. Efficient data structures, in-memory processing, and

optimized networks play roles in achieving low latency.

- **Security:** Protecting data in transit and at rest, and ensuring only authorized entities can produce or consume data.

5.6 Advanced Use Cases

- **Event-Driven Architectures:** Building responsive systems that react to specific data patterns or anomalies.
- **Real-time Analytics:** Powering dashboards that provide live insights into business metrics.
- **Stream-Table Duality:** Bridging the gap between real-time streams and static datasets to provide a holistic view of data.

5.7 Ethical Implications and Best Practices

- **Privacy Concerns:** Streaming personal data, especially without user knowledge, poses significant privacy issues. Compliance with regulations like GDPR and CCPA is essential.

- **Transparency:** Informing stakeholders, especially users, about what data is streamed and how it's used.
- **Data Retention:** Limiting how long data is stored can mitigate potential breaches and privacy concerns.

5.8 Conclusion

Modern data streaming platforms are the backbone of the real-time digital economy. As businesses become increasingly data-driven, the demand for instantaneous insights and reactions will only grow. Understanding the intricacies of data streaming, from technology choices to ethical considerations, is essential for any entity navigating today's digital waters. The subsequent chapters will continue to unravel the tools and strategies that modern businesses employ in their digital arsenal.

Chapter 6: Decentralized Systems and Blockchain

A Deep Dive into the Infrastructure Powering Next-Generation Applications

6.1 The Rise of Decentralization

The digital landscape is undergoing a paradigm shift from centralized to decentralized architectures. Blockchain, often synonymous with decentralization, empowers this transformation. This chapter seeks to unravel the complexities of decentralized systems, examining their potential, challenges, and vast array of applications.

6.2 What is Decentralization?

- **The Centralized Paradigm:** A brief history of centralized digital systems and their inherent limitations.
- **Conceptualizing Decentralization:** Understanding distributed nodes, peer-to-peer interactions, and the lack of a single point of control.
- **Levels of Decentralization:** It's not always absolute; the spectrum ranges from

fully centralized to completely decentralized systems.

6.3 Blockchain: The Poster Child of Decentralization

- **Understanding Blockchain:** A linear, immutable sequence of data blocks interconnected cryptographically.
- **Consensus Mechanisms:** The heart of blockchain's security and trustworthiness, including Proof of Work (PoW) and Proof of Stake (PoS).
- **Smart Contracts:** Automated, self-executing contracts with the terms of agreement written into code.

6.4 Benefits of Decentralized Systems

- **Robustness and Resilience:** With no central point of failure, these systems inherently resist faults and attacks.
- **Transparency and Trust:** Every transaction is visible, creating a trustless environment where participants don't need to know or trust each other.

- **Elimination of Intermediaries:** Direct peer-to-peer interactions can reduce costs and increase efficiency.

6.5 Technical Challenges and Solutions

- **Scalability:** Decentralized systems, especially blockchains, face challenges in handling large volumes of transactions quickly. Solutions include sharding and off-chain transactions.
- **Interoperability:** Ensuring different decentralized platforms can communicate and interact seamlessly.
- **Energy Consumption:** PoW, in particular, is energy-intensive. Alternatives like PoS and hybrid models aim to mitigate this.

6.6 Real-world Applications

- **Cryptocurrencies:** Digital or virtual currencies, like Bitcoin and Ethereum, that use cryptography for security.
- **Supply Chain Management:** Tracking products from origin to consumer, ensuring authenticity and transparency.

- **Decentralized Finance (DeFi):** A new financial system built on public blockchains, offering lending, borrowing, and more without traditional intermediaries.
- **Digital Identity:** Creating tamper-proof digital identities, enhancing security and reducing identity theft.

6.7 Ethical and Regulatory Considerations

- **Privacy Paradox:** While blockchain offers transparency, it can sometimes conflict with individual privacy rights.
- **Regulatory Landscape:** As decentralized systems challenge traditional structures, governments and regulatory bodies are playing catch-up.
- **Potential Misuse:** Like any technology, decentralization can be misused, e.g., in illegal transactions or evading sanctions.

6.8 Conclusion

Decentralized systems, with blockchain at the forefront, are redefining the boundaries of digital possibilities. Their potential to democratize systems, ensure transparency, and resist central control holds promise for a myriad of applications, from finance to healthcare. However, as with all transformative technologies, a judicious blend of innovation, ethics, and governance is essential. The upcoming chapters will continue to explore other revolutionary technologies, laying out the vast tapestry of modern digital infrastructure.

Chapter 7: Edge Computing Paradigms

Shifting the Processing Closer to the Data Source

7.1 The Limitations of Traditional Cloud Computing

Before delving into the intricacies of edge computing, it's crucial to understand the environment from which it emerged. The centralized nature of traditional cloud models, while offering vast storage and compute power, often results in latency and bandwidth inefficiencies.

7.2 Introducing Edge Computing

- **Definition and Principles:** The concept of processing data at the edge of the network, closer to where it's generated, rather than in a centralized cloud-based system.
- **Why the Shift?** The increasing proliferation of IoT devices, the need for real-time processing, and the growing importance of data sovereignty.

7.3 Components of Edge Infrastructure

- **Edge Devices:** These can range from IoT sensors, smartphones, and gateways to more sophisticated devices like drones and autonomous vehicles.
- **Edge Nodes/Clusters:** Localized data centers or micro data centers facilitating computation closer to the data source.
- **Edge Clouds:** Cloud-like capabilities, including orchestration, data analytics, and storage, but located closer to the edge.

7.4 Benefits of Edge Computing

- **Reduced Latency:** Faster data processing and decision-making, crucial for applications like autonomous driving and augmented reality.
- **Bandwidth Efficiency:** By processing data locally, the volume of data sent to centralized data centers is significantly reduced, saving bandwidth.
- **Enhanced Privacy and Security:** Data can be anonymized and processed locally, reducing the risks associated with data transmission.

- **Reliability:** Even if the central server or network fails, edge devices can continue processing locally.

7.5 Challenges in the Edge Ecosystem

- **Complexity:** Managing dispersed and varied devices and nodes can be intricate.
- **Security Concerns:** The vast array of devices can introduce multiple vulnerabilities.
- **Consistency and Synchronization:** Ensuring data integrity and consistency across the edge and central clouds.

7.6 Real-world Applications and Case Studies

- **Healthcare:** Wearables and health monitors that process data in real-time to provide instant feedback or alerts.
- **Retail:** Smart shelves, interactive kiosks, and AR-driven personalized shopping experiences.
- **Smart Cities:** Traffic management, waste management, and energy grid optimization using real-time data from various sensors.

- **Manufacturing:** Predictive maintenance, real-time quality checks, and process optimization in factories.

7.7 The Interplay of Edge Computing with 5G and AI

- **5G:** The next-generation wireless technology, with its low latency and high bandwidth, acts as a catalyst for edge computing deployment.
- **AI at the Edge:** Leveraging machine learning and AI algorithms locally on edge devices for faster insights without the need for centralized processing.

7.8 Ethical and Regulatory Implications

- **Data Sovereignty:** With local processing, data might not leave its jurisdiction, aligning with data residency laws.
- **Surveillance and Privacy:** Edge devices, especially in public spaces, could be misused for unauthorized surveillance, raising ethical questions.

7.9 Conclusion

Edge computing represents a significant evolution in the way data is processed in our increasingly connected world. By shifting computation closer to the data source, edge paradigms promise faster, more efficient, and contextually relevant processing. As digital landscapes become more intricate, understanding and harnessing the potential of edge computing will be paramount. Future chapters will dive deeper into other complementary technologies and trends that are shaping our digital tomorrow.

Chapter 8: Quantum Computing: The Next Frontier

Unveiling the Power of Superposition and Entanglement

8.1 The Classical Computing Landscape

A brief retrospective on classical computing, highlighting the binary nature of bits, the principles of Boolean logic, and the physical limitations of classical processors.

8.2 Introduction to Quantum Computing

- **Quantum Bits (Qubits):** Unlike classical bits that are either 0 or 1, qubits can be in a superposition of both states simultaneously, offering exponential computational power.
- **Entanglement:** A quantum phenomenon where qubits become interlinked and the state of one qubit instantly influences the state of another, no matter the distance between them.

8.3 Key Principles of Quantum Mechanics for Computing

- **Superposition:** The ability of quantum systems to exist in multiple states at once.
- **Quantum Tunneling:** Allows quantum particles to pass through barriers, a phenomenon exploited in certain quantum algorithms.
- **Quantum Interference:** The combination and cancellation of quantum states, crucial for quantum search algorithms.

8.4 The Quantum Advantage

- **Speed:** Quantum algorithms can potentially solve problems in seconds that would take classical computers millennia.
- **Parallelism:** Quantum computers can process a vast amount of possibilities simultaneously.
- **Cryptography:** Quantum systems offer the potential for nearly unbreakable encryption but also pose threats to classical cryptographic methods.

8.5 Challenges in Quantum Computing

- **Error Rates:** Quantum systems are susceptible to interference from their environment, leading to errors.
- **Decoherence:** The fragile state of qubits can easily collapse, limiting the time for quantum computations.
- **Hardware Challenges:** Building stable qubits and maintaining ultra-cold operating temperatures are significant hurdles.

8.6 Quantum Computing Applications

- **Cryptography:** Post-quantum cryptography methods and quantum key distribution for secure communication.
- **Drug Discovery:** Simulating complex molecular structures to discover new drugs.
- **Optimization:** Solving complex optimization problems with applications in logistics, finance, and more.
- **Machine Learning:** Quantum-enhanced machine learning algorithms that can process vast datasets more efficiently.

8.7 Navigating the Quantum vs. Classical Landscape

- **Hybrid Systems:** Leveraging quantum accelerators to enhance classical computing tasks.
- **Quantum Readiness:** Preparing current systems and algorithms for a future where quantum capabilities might be mainstream.

8.8 Ethical and Societal Implications

- **Quantum Hacking:** The potential risks quantum computers pose to existing security protocols and data encryption.
- **Quantum Divide:** The possibility of creating a technological divide between entities that have quantum capabilities and those that don't.

8.9 Conclusion

Quantum computing, while in its infancy, promises a computational revolution. Its potential to redefine sectors like healthcare, finance, and security is unparalleled. However, with great power comes great responsibility. As we stand on the precipice of this quantum leap, understanding its intricacies, potential, and implications is imperative. The subsequent chapters will delve further into how emerging technologies might intersect with, benefit from, or be threatened by the quantum frontier.

Chapter 9: Natural Language Processing (NLP): Making Machines Understand and Generate Human Language

Understanding, Interpreting, and Crafting Human Expressions Digitally

9.1 The Evolution of Human-Computer Interaction

A glimpse into the progression from command-line interfaces to GUIs, and the rising prominence of natural, conversation-based interactions, emphasizing the human desire for intuitive machine interactions.

9.2 What is Natural Language Processing?

- **Defining NLP:** The interdisciplinary domain that bridges linguistics and computing, enabling machines to comprehend, interpret, generate, and respond to human language.
- **NLP Subfields:** Brief introductions to Natural Language Understanding (NLU),

Natural Language Generation (NLG), and Speech Recognition.

9.3 Key Techniques in NLP

- **Tokenization:** Breaking down text into words, phrases, or other meaningful elements.
- **Part-of-Speech Tagging:** Classifying words into their respective parts of speech.
- **Named Entity Recognition:** Identifying and classifying named entities in text into categories such as person names, organizations, or locations.
- **Sentiment Analysis:** Determining the emotional tone or sentiment behind a piece of text.

9.4 Deep Learning in NLP

- **Word Embeddings:** Representations of words in a dense vector form that capture semantic meanings.
- **Recurrent Neural Networks (RNNs) and LSTMs:** Neural network architectures designed to handle sequential data, essential for language.

- **Transformer Architectures:** Introduction to attention mechanisms and architectures like BERT and GPT that have revolutionized NLP tasks.

9.5 Real-world Applications of NLP

- **Chatbots and Virtual Assistants:** Automating customer support and personal assistance using conversational AI.
- **Machine Translation:** Translating text from one language to another, with platforms like Google Translate as exemplars.
- **Text Summarization:** Extracting and generating concise summaries from long pieces of text.
- **Speech Recognition:** Converting spoken language into text, powering voice assistants like Siri and Alexa.

9.6 Challenges in NLP

- **Ambiguity and Context:** The multifaceted nature of language, where words can have varied meanings based on context.

- **Cultural Nuances:** Language is deeply rooted in culture, posing challenges in interpretation and generation for diverse global audiences.
- **Bias and Fairness:** NLP models can inadvertently learn and perpetuate biases present in training data.

9.7 The Ethical Landscape in NLP

- **Data Privacy:** Concerns related to the use and storage of user-generated textual data.
- **Misinformation:** The potential misuse of advanced NLP models in generating fake news or deceptive content.
- **Transparency and Accountability:** Ensuring that NLP models are transparent in their operations and accountable for their outputs.

9.8 Conclusion

Natural Language Processing stands at the crossroads of linguistics and technology, enabling more human-like interactions with machines. Its vast array of applications, from simplifying tasks with virtual assistants to breaking down language barriers, underscores its transformative potential. However, it also carries with it the profound responsibility of ethical and unbiased deployment. As we venture further into the digital age, the symbiosis of man and machine through language will undoubtedly play a pivotal role, a theme recurrent in the forthcoming chapters.

Chapter 10: Blockchain and Decentralized Systems

Redefining Trust and Transactions in a Digital World

10.1 Tracing the Origins of Centralization

A brief overview of centralized systems, their advantages, and inherent vulnerabilities. This includes discussions on single points of failure, trust issues, and centralized control.

10.2 Introducing Blockchain

- **What is Blockchain?** At its core, blockchain is a distributed ledger technology that ensures transparency, immutability, and decentralization.
- **Structure of a Block:** Detailed breakdown of a block's components, including transaction data, timestamp, previous block hash, and its own unique hash.

10.3 Understanding Key Blockchain Concepts

- **Decentralization:** Moving away from a central authority to a distributed network of participants.
- **Consensus Mechanisms:** Protocols like Proof-of-Work (PoW) and Proof-of-Stake (PoS) that ensure all participants agree on the validity of transactions.
- **Cryptography in Blockchain:** The role of cryptographic techniques in ensuring data integrity and participant anonymity.

10.4 Varieties of Blockchain

- **Public vs. Private Blockchains:** Understanding the difference between open, permissionless systems and controlled, permissioned systems.
- **Consortium Blockchains:** Blockchains where a group, rather than a single entity or the public, makes decisions.
- **Sidechains and Layer-2 Solutions:** Techniques and structures to improve scalability and interoperability of blockchains.

10.5 Applications of Blockchain

- **Cryptocurrencies:** Digital or virtual currencies like Bitcoin and Ethereum that use cryptography for security.
- **Smart Contracts:** Self-executing contracts where the terms of agreement are written into code.
- **Supply Chain and Provenance:** Tracking goods transparently throughout their lifecycle.
- **Decentralized Finance (DeFi):** A set of financial applications and platforms built on top of blockchain platforms.

10.6 Challenges and Criticisms of Blockchain

- **Scalability:** The ongoing challenge of processing a high number of transactions quickly.
- **Energy Consumption:** Particularly in blockchains using PoW, the energy used can be immense.
- **Irreversibility:** Once a transaction is added, it can't be reversed, leading to potential issues.

10.7 The Ethical and Regulatory Landscape of Blockchain

- **Decentralization vs. Regulation:** The tug-of-war between the decentralized ethos of blockchain and the need for regulatory oversight.
- **Privacy and Security:** Ensuring user data protection while maintaining the core transparent nature of blockchain.
- **Tokenomics and Fair Distribution:** Concerns related to the fair distribution of tokens in blockchain ecosystems.

10.8 Conclusion

Blockchain and decentralized systems represent a paradigm shift in how data and transactions are managed digitally. They introduce a new layer of trust, transparency, and democratization to digital infrastructures. While they come with transformative potential, especially in sectors like finance, supply chain, and governance, they also introduce new challenges and ethical considerations. As the digital world grapples with questions of trust, centralization, and control, understanding and harnessing blockchain's potential becomes crucial, a theme that will resonate in the subsequent chapters of this guide.

Chapter 11: Edge Computing: Processing at the Source

Driving Responsiveness and Efficiency Closer to Data Origin

11.1 The Centralized Cloud Paradigm

A brief outline of traditional cloud computing, emphasizing centralized data centers' roles in processing vast amounts of data and providing computational services to a global audience.

11.2 Introduction to Edge Computing

- **Defining Edge Computing:** The concept of processing data closer to its source, be it IoT devices, local computers, or edge servers, to reduce latency and enhance efficiency.
- **Contrasting Cloud and Edge:** Understanding the fundamental differences between centralized cloud computing and decentralized edge computing architectures.

11.3 Why Edge Computing Matters

- **Latency Reduction:** The critical role of edge computing in real-time applications where minimal latency is imperative, such as autonomous vehicles and augmented reality.
- **Bandwidth Efficiency:** By processing data locally, edge computing can significantly reduce the amount of data transferred to the cloud, saving bandwidth.
- **Enhanced Privacy and Security:** Local data processing can often keep sensitive data on-premises, reducing exposure to potential breaches.

11.4 Key Components of Edge Computing

- **Edge Devices:** These could range from IoT devices, like sensors and cameras, to more advanced computing hardware.
- **Edge Gateways:** Intermediate processing nodes that aggregate data from multiple edge devices and can also run localized computations.
- **Network Infrastructure:** The optimized networking solutions that ensure seamless data flow between edge components and centralized data centers.

11.5 Challenges in Edge Computing

- **Device Heterogeneity:** The vast variety of edge devices, each with its capabilities and specifications, can pose compatibility and standardization issues.
- **Security Concerns:** The distributed nature of edge computing can introduce multiple points of vulnerability.
- **Resource Constraints:** Unlike massive centralized data centers, edge devices often have limited computational resources.

11.6 Real-world Applications of Edge Computing

- **Healthcare Monitoring:** Using local devices to monitor patient vitals in real-time, with immediate local processing to alert medical professionals.
- **Smart Cities:** Leveraging edge devices for traffic monitoring, energy management, and urban planning without overwhelming central servers.
- **Retail and Customer Experience:** Using edge computing to provide real-time, personalized offers to shoppers or to manage inventory efficiently.

11.7 The Future of Edge and Cloud Synergy

- **Fog Computing:** Bridging the gap between cloud and edge, fog computing involves an intermediate layer of processing nodes to balance efficiency and computational power.
- **Multi-access Edge Computing (MEC):** Integrating edge computing into mobile networks to enhance user experiences and responsiveness.
- **Serverless Edge:** The potential for deploying on-demand functions at the edge, only when needed, aligning with the serverless computing paradigm.

11.8 Conclusion

Edge computing, by bringing processing closer to data origin, offers a complementary approach to the traditional cloud paradigm. It holds immense potential in a world that is becoming increasingly interconnected, with billions of devices generating zettabytes of data. As applications demand more immediacy and data privacy becomes paramount, the edge will play a critical role in shaping the digital landscape. In upcoming chapters, the interplay of various technologies with edge computing will further elucidate its foundational importance in the modern tech ecosystem.

Chapter 12: Quantum Computing: A Leap into the Future of Computation

Exploiting Quantum Mechanics to Solve Previously Insurmountable Problems

12.1 Traditional Computing: A Brief Recap

A concise review of classical computing principles, focusing on binary data representation using bits and the deterministic nature of classical algorithms.

12.2 Introducing Quantum Mechanics

- **Wave-Particle Duality:** The foundational principle wherein particles can exhibit both wave-like and particle-like properties.
- **Superposition:** Unlike classical bits that are either 0 or 1, quantum bits (qubits) can exist in a superposition of states.
- **Entanglement:** A unique quantum phenomenon where qubits become intertwined, such that the state of one qubit is dependent on another, regardless of the distance between them.

12.3 Principles of Quantum Computing

- **Qubits:** The quantum equivalent of bits, offering a more versatile and dynamic representation of information.
- **Quantum Gates:** Operations that manipulate qubits, akin to logic gates in classical computing but more intricate due to the complexities of quantum mechanics.
- **Quantum Entropy and Decoherence:** Challenges in maintaining stable qubit states over time, with decoherence being a primary obstacle to scalable quantum computing.

12.4 Potential Quantum Computing Applications

- **Cryptography:** Quantum computers can potentially break several cryptographic protocols currently considered secure, necessitating the development of quantum-resistant algorithms.
- **Drug Discovery:** Quantum algorithms could simulate complex molecular and chemical reactions, accelerating drug development.

- **Optimization Problems:** Tasks like the traveling salesman problem or integer factorization could see significant speed-up with quantum algorithms.

12.5 Challenges in Quantum Computing

- **Error Rates:** Quantum computations are currently error-prone, requiring techniques like quantum error correction to maintain accuracy.
- **Scalability:** Developing large-scale, stable quantum computers remains a technological challenge.
- **Hardware Varieties:** Different quantum computing approaches, from trapped ions to superconducting qubits, each with their benefits and hurdles.

12.6 Quantum vs. Classical: A Comparative Analysis

- **Speed:** While certain problems can be solved exponentially faster on quantum computers, others might not see as significant an advantage.
- **Versatility:** Quantum computers are not general-purpose machines but are

specifically designed for problems that classical computers struggle with.

- **Integration:** The potential synergies between quantum and classical systems in hybrid computational approaches.

12.7 The Ethical and Security Implications of Quantum Computing

- **Data Security:** The challenge of redefining encryption in a post-quantum world.
- **Economic Impacts:** Potential disruptions in industries unprepared for quantum advancements.
- **Quantum Supremacy:** The milestone where quantum computers outperform classical machines in specific tasks and its broader implications.

12.8 Conclusion

Quantum computing, while still in its nascent stages, promises to redefine the boundaries of what is computationally feasible. By harnessing the peculiarities of quantum mechanics, it opens doors to problems once deemed unsolvable. However, with its vast potential come significant challenges, both technical and ethical. As we navigate the quantum era, a comprehensive understanding of its implications is paramount, setting the tone for the next chapters that delve deeper into the interplay of emerging technologies.

Chapter 13: Augmented Reality (AR) and Virtual Reality (VR): Bridging Real and Virtual Domains

Evolving Human-Computer Interactions and Shaping Immersive Experiences

13.1 Tracing Back the Origins

A retrospective glance at early endeavors to merge reality with digital information, and the visionaries who set the stage for modern AR and VR.

13.2 Defining AR and VR

- **Augmented Reality (AR):** The enhancement of real-world environments by overlaying them with digital information or imagery.
- **Virtual Reality (VR):** A fully immersive experience wherein users are transported into a simulated environment, detached from the real world.

13.3 Key Components of AR and VR Systems

- **Display Technologies:** From head-mounted displays (HMD) to AR smart glasses, understanding the hardware that renders AR and VR content.
- **Tracking and Sensing:** How AR and VR systems perceive user movement and interactions, enabling responsive feedback.
- **Rendering and Simulation:** The computational processes that generate and refresh the virtual imagery in real-time.

13.4 The Multifaceted Applications of AR and VR

- **Gaming and Entertainment:** The realms where VR has achieved significant traction, offering deeply immersive experiences.
- **Industrial Design and Prototyping:** Using AR and VR for product visualization and iterative design without physical prototypes.
- **Medical Training and Therapy:** Simulated surgeries, patient care scenarios, and even therapeutic VR environments to treat conditions like PTSD.

- **Real Estate and Architecture:** Virtual property tours and structural visualizations before constructions commence.

13.5 Challenges Confronting AR and VR

- **Hardware Limitations:** The quest for lighter, more comfortable, and more affordable display systems.
- **Latency and Motion Sickness:** The need to reduce lag to prevent user discomfort and ensure a seamless experience.
- **Content Creation:** As the hardware evolves, there's an increasing demand for high-quality AR and VR content.

13.6 Social and Ethical Considerations

- **Digital Dependency:** The potential consequences of blurring the lines between the real and virtual worlds.
- **Data Privacy:** As AR and VR systems capture more about users, from movements to biometric data, issues of consent and data misuse arise.

- **Accessibility and Inclusivity:** Ensuring AR and VR technologies are universally accessible and cater to diverse user needs.

13.7 Emerging Trends and the Road Ahead

- **Mixed Reality (MR):** Merging AR and VR to interact with both real-world and digital objects.
- **Haptic Feedback:** Integrating tactile sensations into AR and VR experiences.
- **AI Integration:** Leveraging artificial intelligence to enhance the realism and responsiveness of virtual environments.

13.8 Conclusion

AR and VR technologies, while distinctly different, both offer transformative potential in how we perceive and interact with digital content. They redefine the paradigms of human-computer interaction and hold the promise of more intuitive, immersive, and personal digital experiences. As we venture further into the digital age, understanding the intricacies, possibilities, and challenges of AR and VR becomes indispensable, paving the way for the ensuing discussions in this guide.

Chapter 14: Blockchain and Distributed Ledger Technology: Trusting the Immutable

Securing Transactions and Records in a Decentralized World

14.1 The Genesis of Blockchain

A brief recount of the inception of blockchain technology, emphasizing its debut with the creation of Bitcoin and the vision of a decentralized currency system.

14.2 Understanding Blockchain and Distributed Ledgers

- **The Block:** Each block contains a timestamp, transaction data, and a reference to the previous block, ensuring a linked chain of records.
- **Decentralization:** Unlike centralized databases, blockchain operates over a network of computers, each holding a copy of the entire blockchain.
- **Consensus Mechanisms:** Processes such as Proof-of-Work (PoW) and Proof-of-

Stake (PoS) that ensure all participants agree on the validity of transactions.

14.3 Cryptography: The Backbone of Blockchain

- **Hash Functions:** Creating unique outputs (hashes) for varying inputs and ensuring data integrity.
- **Public and Private Keys:** A pair of cryptographic keys, wherein the public key is open to all, and the private key remains confidential.
- **Digital Signatures:** Ensuring transaction authenticity and proving the ownership of digital assets.

14.4 Advantages and Use Cases of Blockchain

- **Transparency and Traceability:** Every transaction is recorded and accessible, leading to enhanced auditability and accountability.
- **Smart Contracts:** Self-executing contracts where terms and conditions are written in code, ensuring automatic fulfillment upon meeting criteria.

- **Supply Chain Management:** Tracking goods from their origin to consumption, ensuring authenticity and preventing fraud.
- **Decentralized Finance (DeFi):** Creating financial systems without intermediaries, from loans to asset trading.

14.5 Challenges in the Blockchain Realm

- **Scalability:** As the chain grows, ensuring speedy transactions becomes challenging.
- **Energy Consumption:** Certain consensus mechanisms, especially PoW, consume vast amounts of energy.
- **Interoperability:** With multiple blockchain platforms, ensuring seamless interaction between them is a challenge.

14.6 Ethical and Regulatory Implications

- **Data Immutability vs. Right to Erasure:** In a world of GDPR and data rights, the permanent nature of blockchain records poses dilemmas.
- **Decentralization vs. Regulation:** Striking a balance between a decentralized ethos and the need for regulatory oversight.

- **Tokenization and Asset Ownership:** Ensuring that tokenized assets, from art to real estate, have a legitimate backing in the real world.

14.7 Emerging Trends in Blockchain

- **Layer 2 Solutions:** Technologies built on top of existing blockchains to enhance scalability and efficiency.
- **Cross-Chain Platforms:** Facilitating communication and transactions between different blockchain networks.
- **Quantum-Resistant Blockchains:** Preparing for a world where quantum computing could challenge current cryptographic methods.

14.8 Conclusion

Blockchain, with its foundational principles of decentralization, transparency, and security, has shown potential far beyond just digital currencies. It offers a reimagined architecture for trust in the digital age. As industries grapple with the challenges of integration and adaptation, understanding blockchain's nuances and transformative potential becomes imperative.

This chapter sets the stage for subsequent discussions on how emerging technologies can interweave with and be enhanced by blockchain principles.

Chapter 15: Machine Learning and Deep Learning: Machines That Learn and Evolve

Decoding the Algorithms Powering Intelligent Systems

15.1 Setting the Stage: The Rise of Machine Learning

A brief historical overview of machine learning, tracing its roots from early algorithms to its prominence in today's digital landscape.

15.2 The Fundamentals of Machine Learning

- **Supervised Learning:** Algorithms that learn from labeled training data, making predictions based on this data.
- **Unsupervised Learning:** Algorithms that identify patterns and structures in unlabelled data.
- **Reinforcement Learning:** Algorithms that learn by interacting with an environment, optimizing for a reward signal.

15.3 Deep Learning: Going Deeper into the Data

- **Neural Networks:** Architectures inspired by human brain neurons, processing data in layers to extract features and patterns.
- **Convolutional Neural Networks (CNNs):** Specialized for processing structured grid data like images.
- **Recurrent Neural Networks (RNNs):** Designed for sequential data, having memory of previous computations.

15.4 Key Applications and Breakthroughs

- **Image and Speech Recognition:** How machine learning models can recognize patterns in visual and auditory data.
- **Natural Language Processing:** Understanding and generating human language, driving advancements in chatbots and translation tools.
- **Healthcare Diagnostics:** Predicting diseases and analyzing medical images with higher precision.
- **Autonomous Vehicles:** Machine learning at the core of self-driving

algorithms, understanding and reacting to complex environments.

15.5 Challenges and Limitations

- **Data Dependency:** The need for vast amounts of data for training sophisticated models.
- **Overfitting:** When a model is too attuned to the training data and performs poorly on unseen data.
- **Interpretability:** The 'black box' nature of some deep learning models, making it challenging to interpret their decision-making process.

15.6 Ethical Considerations in Machine Learning

- **Bias and Fairness:** Ensuring that algorithms don't perpetuate or amplify societal biases present in training data.
- **Privacy Concerns:** Balancing model efficiency with user data privacy, especially with models deployed in the public domain.
- **Automation and Job Displacement:** Addressing the societal impacts of tasks

being replaced by machine learning-driven systems.

15.7 Future Horizons and Emerging Innovations

- **Few-Shot and Zero-Shot Learning:** Training models effectively with limited data.
- **Neural Architecture Search:** Algorithms that search for the best-performing neural network architecture for a specific task.
- **Edge AI:** Bringing machine learning computations closer to data sources, like IoT devices, reducing the need for centralized processing.

15.8 Conclusion

Machine learning, particularly its deep learning subset, stands at the forefront of technological innovation, ushering in a new era where machines not only compute but also "understand" and "learn". As businesses, governments, and individuals increasingly rely on these technologies, a nuanced grasp of their capabilities, challenges, and broader implications becomes essential. This foundational knowledge prepares readers for subsequent chapters that delve deeper into the symbiotic relationship between machine learning and other emerging domains.

Chapter 16: Internet of Things (IoT): A Connected World of Devices

Transforming Everyday Objects into Smart Entities

16.1 The IoT Genesis: From Internet to Things

A chronological recap of how connectivity evolved from computers to everyday objects, marking the dawn of the IoT era.

16.2 What Defines IoT?

- **Device Connectivity:** The fundamental principle where devices, from refrigerators to industrial sensors, connect to the internet.
- **Data Exchange:** Devices in the IoT ecosystem don't just connect; they exchange data, contributing to a vast digital information pool.
- **Smart Interactions:** Beyond connectivity and data exchange, these devices "act" based on the data they receive, often autonomously.

16.3 Components of an IoT System

- **Sensors and Actuators:** The physical components that detect changes in the environment or perform actions.
- **Connectivity:** Using technologies like Wi-Fi, Bluetooth, and LoRaWAN, devices connect to networks or other devices.
- **Data Processing:** Often done in cloud-based systems, this involves analyzing the data collected by IoT devices.
- **User Interface:** The platforms through which humans can interact with IoT devices, such as apps or web portals.

16.4 Pioneering Applications of IoT

- **Smart Homes:** Systems that automate lighting, security, and even thermostats, optimizing for energy usage and user comfort.
- **Wearable Health Devices:** Watches and bands that monitor health metrics and provide real-time feedback.
- **Industrial IoT (IIoT):** Machinery and tools that predict maintenance needs and streamline manufacturing processes.

- **Smart Cities:** Urban environments with connected traffic lights, waste management systems, and public utilities for optimized city management.

16.5 Challenges in the IoT Landscape

- **Security Concerns:** The increasing number of connected devices provides more entry points for cyber-attacks.
- **Interoperability:** Ensuring different devices from various manufacturers can seamlessly interact.
- **Data Management:** Handling the massive amounts of data generated without overwhelming storage and processing systems.

16.6 Ethical and Social Implications

- **Privacy:** As devices collect more personal data, concerns arise about who can access this information and how it's used.
- **Over-reliance on Technology:** The balance between enjoying the conveniences of IoT and not becoming overly dependent.
- **Environmental Impact:** Addressing the environmental cost of producing, using,

and disposing of a vast number of connected devices.

16.7 Glimpsing the Future: Advanced IoT Innovations

- **Edge Computing:** Processing data closer to where it's generated rather than relying on centralized cloud systems.
- **5G and IoT:** How the advent of 5G networks will turbocharge the capabilities and applications of IoT.
- **Quantum IoT:** Leveraging the potential of quantum computing in enhancing IoT functions and security.

16.8 Conclusion

The Internet of Things, with its vision of a seamlessly connected world, holds transformative potential across sectors. It embodies a paradigm where the distinction between the digital and physical realms blurs. Grasping its mechanisms, applications, and challenges is pivotal as we navigate an increasingly interconnected future. The knowledge gained from this chapter will be instrumental when exploring the integrative potential of IoT with other cutting-edge technologies in subsequent discussions.

Chapter 17: Augmented Reality (AR) and Virtual Reality (VR): Bridging the Virtual and Real Worlds

The Convergence of Digital Perception and Physical Experience

17.1 Introduction: The Digital Lens on Reality

An overview of the transformative journey from early computer graphics to the immersive experiences offered by today's AR and VR technologies.

17.2 Fundamentals of AR and VR

- **Virtual Reality (VR):** Completely immersive digital environments that transport users away from their actual surroundings.
- **Augmented Reality (AR):** Overlays digital content onto the real world, enhancing one's current perception of reality.

17.3 Hardware and Software Pioneers

- **Headsets and Glasses:** Devices such as the Oculus Rift, HTC Vive, and Microsoft HoloLens that have redefined immersive experiences.
- **Motion Controllers and Haptics:** Tools that allow users to interact with and feel the virtual environment.
- **Development Platforms:** Frameworks like ARKit, ARCore, and Unity, empowering developers to craft AR and VR applications.

17.4 Revolutionary Applications

- **Gaming and Entertainment:** From augmented Pokémon hunts to virtual spaceship battles, reshaping the entertainment sector.
- **Education and Training:** Immersive environments for teaching everything from history to surgical procedures.
- **Real Estate and Architecture:** Virtual property tours and augmented architectural visualizations.
- **Retail and Fashion:** Virtual try-ons and interactive shopping experiences.

17.5 Technological Challenges and Barriers

- **Latency Issues:** The importance of real-time response in immersive environments to prevent motion sickness.
- **Field of View (FOV):** Expanding the visual range in AR glasses to enhance user experience.
- **Hardware Limitations:** Balancing device weight, battery life, and processing power for optimal performance.

17.6 Ethical and Societal Implications

- **Digital Dependency:** The psychological impacts of prolonged immersion in virtual environments.
- **Data Privacy:** Handling the vast amounts of personal data AR and VR systems can collect.
- **Digital Divide:** Ensuring equal access to AR and VR technologies across socioeconomic strata.

17.7 Future Visions: Beyond Today's AR and VR

- **Mixed Reality (MR):** A blend of AR and VR, offering interactive digital elements anchored in the real world.

- **Brain-Computer Interfaces (BCI) in VR:** Direct interfacing of neural activities with virtual environments for unparalleled immersion.
- **Spatial Computing:** Environments where computing is integrated into the world around us, and interactions are spatial and intuitive.

17.8 Conclusion

Augmented and Virtual Realities represent more than just technological innovations; they're gateways to alternate dimensions of experience, merging the tangible with the digital. As these technologies advance and become integrated into our daily lives, understanding their mechanisms, potentials, and challenges is paramount. This chapter sets the foundation for the subsequent exploration of how AR and VR intersect with and amplify other digital frontiers.

Chapter 18: Quantum Computing: Unveiling the Power of Quantum Mechanics

The Leap from Classical Bits to Quantum Bits

18.1 The Quantum Premise: A Brief Overview

An introduction to the quantum world, emphasizing its departure from classical physics and its implications for computation.

18.2 From Classical Bits to Quantum Bits (Qubits)

- **Classical Bits:** The binary building blocks of traditional computing, representing either 0 or 1.
- **Qubits:** Operating on the principles of superposition and entanglement, they can represent both 0 and 1 simultaneously and link their states with other qubits.

18.3 Quantum Gates and Circuits

- **Quantum Gates:** The counterparts to classical logic gates, handling operations on qubits.
- **Building Quantum Circuits:** How quantum gates combine to process information and execute quantum algorithms.

18.4 Key Quantum Algorithms

- **Shor's Algorithm:** A quantum procedure for integer factorization, posing threats to classical cryptographic systems.
- **Grover's Algorithm:** Offering faster searching capabilities for unsorted databases compared to classical counterparts.
- **Quantum Machine Learning Algorithms:** Leveraging quantum parallelism to speed up certain data processing tasks.

18.5 Quantum Computing's Challenges

- **Decoherence and Noise:** Managing the delicate quantum states of qubits against external interference.

- **Error Correction:** Techniques developed to correct inevitable mistakes in quantum calculations.
- **Scaling Difficulties:** The challenge of building large-scale, practical quantum computers.

18.6 The Potential Impact on Industries

- **Cryptography:** The risks and opportunities quantum computing brings to encryption.
- **Drug Discovery:** Harnessing quantum mechanics to model complex molecular and chemical reactions.
- **Optimization Problems:** Addressing challenges in logistics, finance, and AI with quantum-enhanced algorithms.

18.7 Ethical and Social Implications

- **Quantum Security Threats:** Addressing the vulnerabilities posed by quantum capabilities in cybersecurity.
- **Workforce Transition:** Preparing for shifts in job landscapes as quantum computing potentially disrupts certain industries.

- **Access and Equity:** Ensuring that the benefits and capabilities of quantum technology are distributed equitably.

18.8 Looking Forward: The Quantum-Classic Coexistence

- **Hybrid Systems:** How quantum computers can work in tandem with classical systems to address specific challenges.
- **Quantum Networking:** The emergence of ultra-secure quantum communication systems.
- **The Road to Quantum Supremacy:** The ongoing journey towards achieving a quantum system that outperforms the best classical computers in specific tasks.

18.8 Conclusion

Quantum computing, with its roots deep in the principles of quantum mechanics, represents one of the most significant paradigm shifts in the history of computation. Its potential to redefine industries, from finance to healthcare, underscores the importance of a comprehensive understanding of its capabilities and challenges.

With this knowledge, one can navigate the dawning quantum era with clarity and vision, linking its advancements to the broader technological landscape outlined in this book.

Conclusion

Navigating the Digital Horizon - The Symphony of Technological Innovations

The Harmonious Interplay of Technologies

As we've journeyed through the myriad facets of modern technology, from the digital touchpoints of e-commerce systems to the ethereal realms of virtual reality, and from the instantaneous data exchanges in 5G networks to the probabilistic world of quantum computing, one theme stands clear: technology does not exist in isolation. Each innovation, each leap forward, is but a note in a grand symphony of technological progress.

A Mosaic of Possibilities

Every chapter we delved into illustrated not just an isolated domain but also its potential intersections with others. How might quantum computing revolutionize data processing in IoT networks? Could augmented reality enhance our interactions with AI-driven systems? The combinations are near limitless, and each intersection offers a mosaic of possibilities that could redefine our world.

Challenges: The Other Side of Progress

With progress comes responsibility. The challenges – ethical, societal, and technical – highlighted throughout this book are not mere stumbling blocks but rather signposts guiding the way to responsible innovation. Addressing issues of privacy, security, equity, and more ensures that our technological future is not just advanced, but also inclusive and safe.

Preparing for the Future

Understanding is the first step to preparation. The insights shared in this guide aim to arm its readers with the knowledge and foresight to navigate the rapid currents of technological change. Whether one is an industry professional, a tech enthusiast, or a curious onlooker, grappling with these concepts is paramount in an increasingly digital age.

The Continuous Journey

While this book provides a snapshot of the technological landscape as of its last update, the realm of tech is ever-evolving. New innovations, challenges, and intersections will emerge, and the horizon will continually expand. Engaging with technology is, thus, not a destination but a continuous journey.

In Closing

As the digital dawn gives way to the noon of interconnected technologies, we stand at the cusp of unparalleled possibilities. It's an era where our virtual avatars can interact in digitized realms, where our homes respond to our needs before we even articulate them, and where computing is no longer just binary but quantum.

With knowledge as our compass and curiosity as our guide, we can traverse this intricate digital tapestry, unlocking potentials and charting courses to a brighter, interconnected future. Thank you for joining us on this exploration. The next chapters in this grand narrative of technological progress await your contribution.

Printed by BoD™in Norderstedt, Germany

9 781806 218066